BIG DOGS

SAINT BERNARDS

by Nikki Bruno Clapper

Content Consultant: Sarah K. Crain
Doctor of Veterinary Medicine
Tufts University
North Grafton, Massachusetts

Pebble® Plus

CAPSTONE PRESS
a capstone imprint

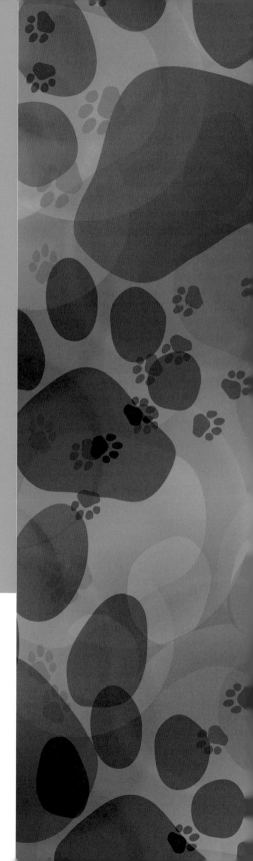

Pebble Plus is published by Capstone Press,
1710 Roe Crest Drive, North Mankato, Minnesota 56003
www.mycapstone.com

Library of Congress Cataloging-in-Publication Data
Cataloging-in-Publication data is on file with the Library of Congress.
ISBN 978-1-4914-7977-3 (library binding)
ISBN 978-1-4914-8561-3 (ebook PDF)

Editorial Credits
Nikki Bruno Clapper, editor; Juliette Peters, designer;
Morgan Walters, media researcher; Katy LaVigne, production specialist

Photo Credits
Alamy: Purestock, 17; iStockphoto: Roberto A Sanchez, 9; Shutterstock: andrewvec, (speedometer)
cover, dezi, 13, DragoNika, 5, Eric Isselee, (dog) bottom left 22, Hywit Dimyadi, (dog silouette)
cover, kostolom3000, (dog head) backcover, 3, Lenkadan, 19, Rita Kochmarjova, 1, 11, 15, 21,
Stephaniellen, (elephant) bottom right 22, tobkatrina, cover, vlastas, (paw prints) design element
throughout; SuperStock: Jean-Michel Labat/ardea.com/Pantheon, 7

Note to Parents and Teachers

The Big Dogs set supports national science standards related to life science. This book describes
and illustrates Saint Bernards. The images support early readers in understanding the text. The
repetition of words and phrases helps early readers learn new words. This book also introduces
early readers to subject-specific vocabulary words, which are defined in the Glossary section. Early
readers may need assistance to read some words and to use the Table of Contents, Glossary, Read
More, Internet Sites, Critical Thinking Using the Common Core, and Index sections of the book.

Printed in the United States of America in North Mankato, Minnesota.
102015   009221CGS16

Table of Contents

Saints to the Rescue 4

Head and Shoulders 10

Caring for a Saint Bernard 14

Glossary 22

Read More 23

Internet Sites 23

Critical Thinking Using
    the Common Core. 24

Index 24

SAINTS TO THE RESCUE

Saint Bernards are

big, strong, and lovable.

They are called Saints

for short. Saints are famous

for rescuing people.

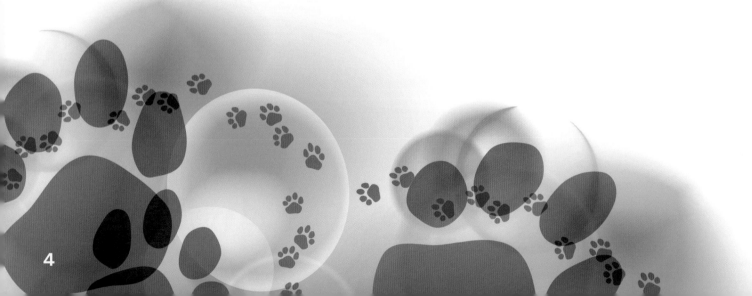

Saint Bernards were bred as working dogs. They rescued lost people in the mountains. They could smell people trapped under the snow.

Today most Saints are pets.
They are friendly with
people and other animals.
Saints are caring and patient
with children.

HEAD AND SHOULDERS

The front part of a Saint's body is huge. It has a big head, a thick neck, and strong shoulders. Its eyes are dark and small.

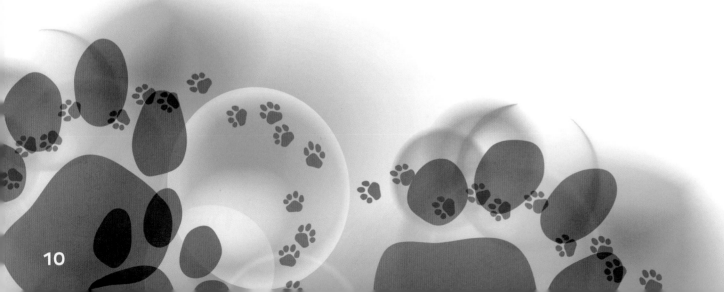

Saint Bernard coats can be long or short. Either way, the coat is thick. Most Saints are white, black, and red or brown.

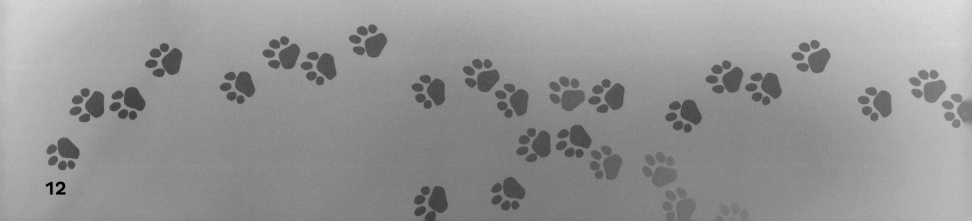

long coat

CARING FOR A SAINT BERNARD

Saints need plenty of care.

Puppies must be trained

not to jump or step

on people. Heavy dogs

can hurt people by mistake.

Grooming a Saint is a big job. They shed lots of hair, and their nails grow fast. You must brush their teeth and clean their drool!

Saint Bernards are

not very active dogs.

But they need daily walks

and playtime. Healthy Saints

live for 10 to 12 years.

Saint Bernards take up
lots of space in your house
and in your car. But many
families are glad to make
room for this sweet pet!

GLOSSARY

breed—to mate and produce young

coat—an animal's hair or fur

daily—happening every day

drool—spit that drips from the mouth

groom—to clean and make an animal look neat

mistake—something done incorrectly

patient—calm during frustrating, difficult times

rescue—to save someone who is in danger

train—to teach an animal to do what you say

working dog—a dog that is bred to do a job, such as rescuing people or herding animals

HOW BIG ARE THEY?

	Saint Bernard	Baby Elephant
Average Height	26–30 inches (66–76 centimeters)	36 inches (91 cm)
Average Weight	120–200 pounds (54–91 kilograms)	200 pounds (91 kg)

42
36
30
24
18
12
6
0

READ MORE

Landau, Elaine. *Saint Bernards Are the Best!* The Best Dogs Ever. Minneapolis, Minn.: Lerner, 2011.

Nelson, Maria. *Saint Bernards.* Great Big Dogs. New York: Gareth Stevens Pub., 2012.

Rudolph, Jessica. *Saint Bernard: Mountain Rescuer.* Big Dogs Rule. New York: Bearport Pub., 2012.

INTERNET SITES

FactHound offers a safe, fun way to find Internet sites related to this book. All of the sites on FactHound have been researched by our staff.

Here's all you do:

Visit *www.facthound.com*

Type in this code: 9781491479773

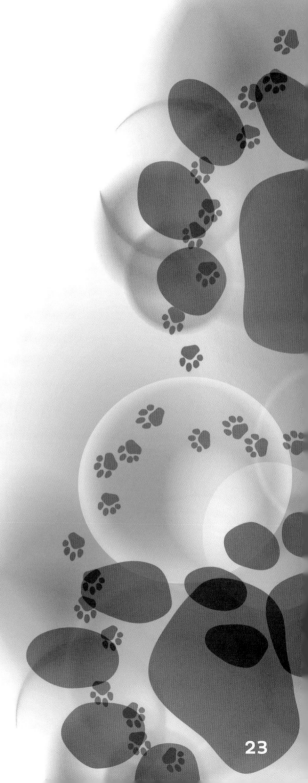

Check out projects, games and lots more at
www.capstonekids.com

CRITICAL THINKING
USING THE COMMON CORE

1. What types of grooming does a Saint Bernard need?
   (Key Ideas and Details)

2. Why do you think Saint Bernards are good family pets?
   (Integration of Knowledge and Ideas)

INDEX

body, 10
care, 14, 16, 18
children, 8
coat, 12
colors, 12

grooming, 16
life span, 18
pet, 8, 20
rescue, 4, 6
training, 14